D0623117

DATE DUE			
FEB 8			

LIFE

ORIGINS AND EVOLUTION

EVOLUTION OF THE UNIVERSE

4.5 billion years ago the oceans and first landmasses form.

9

1 million years after the Big Bang, hydrogen atoms form.

5

10-20 billion years ago, in less than a second, four things happen.

1. The Big Bang
2. Inflation
3. The beginning of the four forces
4. The first atomic nuclei form

1 billion years after the Big Bang, galaxies begin to form.

6

8　4.6 billion years ago
the Earth's crust forms.

7　5 billion years ago
the planet Earth forms.

11　2.5 billion years ago
the atmosphere forms.

10　3 billion years ago
bacteria appear—
life begins.

BEGINNINGS

LIFE
ORIGINS AND EVOLUTION

by
Alessandro Garassino

English Translation by Rocco Serini

RSVP
**RAINTREE
STECK-VAUGHN**
P U B L I S H E R S
The Steck-Vaughn Company

Austin, Texas

Published by Raintree Steck-Vaughn Publishers, an imprint of Steck-Vaughn Company

Series Editor: Caterina Longanesi
American Edition, Edit and Rewrite: Susan Wilson
Consultant: Yaakov Shechter, Lehman College, The City University of New York
Project Manager: Julie Klaus
Electronic Production: Scott Melcer
Cover Artwork: Antonio Molino

Photographs: Alessandro Boesi, Milan: p. 29 (9), p. 34 (5,6). Duilio Citi, Chiavari: p. 35 (8). Alberto Contri, Milan: p. 32-33 (Doberman, Great Dane, 4), p. 38 (3), p. 39 (5). Editoriale Jaca Book, Milan (Carlo Scotti): p. 10 (2, 3), p. 11 (4), p. 30-31 (leaves and petals in amber; ammonite: first, third, fifth from left; fossilized trunk), p. 32-33 (bobtail, husky), p. 34 (3). F. Heinze/ Grazia Neri, Milan: p. 33 (6). Paolo Longanesi, Milano: p. 33 (bulldog). Nasa: p. 41 (2, 3). Giovanni Pinna, Milan: p. 31 (gecko in amber). Giorgio Teruzzi, Milan: p. 17 (3), p. 30-31 (ammonite: second and fourth from the left).

Illustrations: Ettore Antonini, Milan: p. 25 (3). Editoriale Jaca Book, Milan (Maria Elena Gonano): p. 18-19, p. 26-27, p. 28-29, p. 33 (2-3), p. 36-37; (Rosalba Moriggia): p. 8-9, p. 12 (2), p. 14-15, p. 16 (1, 2), p. 17 (4), p. 20 (1), p. 22-23, p. 24 (1, 2, 4, 5), p. 25 (6), p. 34 (1, 2), p. 40 (1); (Maria Piatto): p. 10, (1), p. 12 (1), p. 21 (3, 4).
Illustration p. 20 (2) Francis Leroy, *L'origine de la vie*, Editions Biocosmos Centre/Francis Leroy, 1993, p. 71.

Graphics and Layout: The Graphics Department of Jaca Book
Special thanks to the Museum of Natural History of Milan

Library of Congress Cataloging-in-Publication Data
Garassino, Alessandro.
  [Vita. English]
  Life: origins and evolution / by Alessandro Garassino; illustrated by Maria Elena Gonano, Rosalba Moriggia, Maria Piatto; translated by Rocco Serini.
     p.   cm. — (Beginnings)
  Includes index.
  ISBN 0-8114-3335-8
  1. Evolution (Biology) — Juvenile literature. 2. Life — Origin — Juvenile literature.
  [1. Evolution. 2. Life — Origin.] I. Gonano, Maria Elena, ill. II. Moriggia, Rosalba, ill.
  III. Piatto, Maria, ill. IV. Title. V. Series. Beginnings (Austin, Tex.)
  QH367.1.G3813   1995
  57—dc20   94-8582
                                                                   CIP
                                                                   AC

Printed and bound in the United States

1 2 3 4 5 6 7 8 9 0 KP 99 98 97 96 95 94

TABLE OF CONTENTS

THE TUNNEL OF TIME

At one time people thought that plants and animals simply appeared on Earth—that the Earth was suddenly populated with these different types of living things. But as scientists looked more closely at living organisms, they found many common traits. They found connections between all living things. And they began to ask if one type of living thing led to another.

One trait of all living things is to take in nutrients and give off wastes. Even plants that make their own food take in materials in order to do this. Living things also respond to their surroundings—if they did not they would die. In addition, all living things grow and reproduce, or make more of their own kind.

Over the years, scientists found more traits common among all living things. For example, all living things are made up of cells. Inside the cells of all living things, from the simplest bacteria to the most complex animals, are many of the same chemicals. One of these is a molecule that directs the cell. This same molecule is copied and transferred to new cells as cells reproduce. This important molecule is known by its initials, DNA. You will learn more about it later in this book.

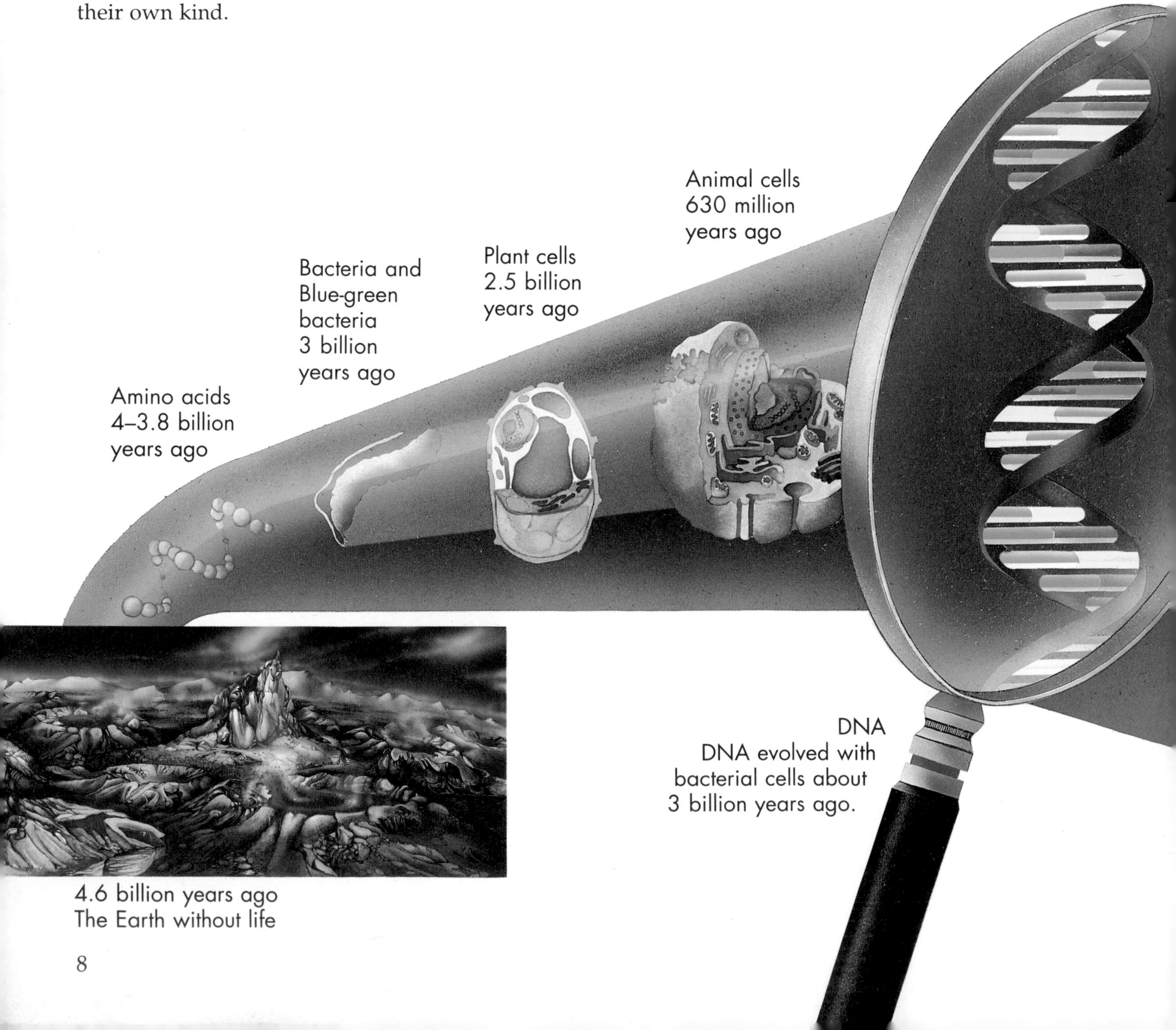

Animal cells
630 million
years ago

Plant cells
2.5 billion
years ago

Bacteria and
Blue-green
bacteria
3 billion
years ago

Amino acids
4–3.8 billion
years ago

DNA
DNA evolved with
bacterial cells about
3 billion years ago.

4.6 billion years ago
The Earth without life

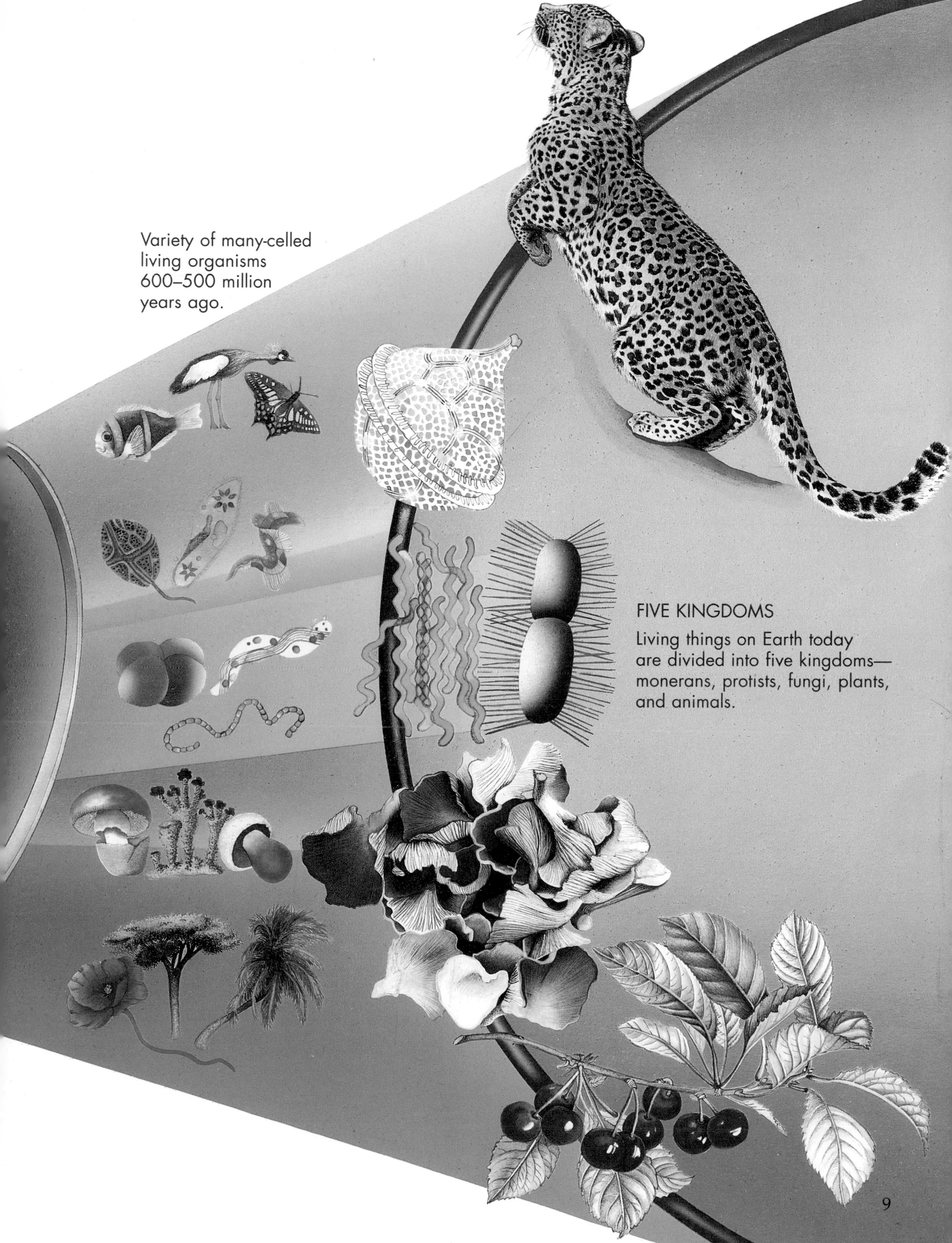

Variety of many-celled
living organisms
600–500 million
years ago.

FIVE KINGDOMS

Living things on Earth today
are divided into five kingdoms—
monerans, protists, fungi, plants,
and animals.

THE EARTH WITHOUT LIFE

In the beginning, the Earth had no life. Our planet was simply a molten mass of rock. On its surface were swirling seas of molten rock. Not only was there no life, there was no land, no ocean, not even an **atmosphere**.

But in time the surface of the Earth began to cool. And the molten rock began to harden into solid rock. As it hardened, it formed the crust—a hard shell making up the Earth's outer layer. But beneath this rigid shell, most of the planet was still a churning mass of molten rock. As the rock moved, it would cause cracks to form in the crust above. Through these cracks, volcanoes would erupt, sending out more molten rock to the Earth's surface.

Molten rock was not the only substance to spew out of the volcanoes. Gases trapped inside the Earth also came bursting to the surface. As these gases rose above the surface, they formed a blanket around the Earth—a forbidding atmosphere of carbon monoxide, ammonia, and water vapor.

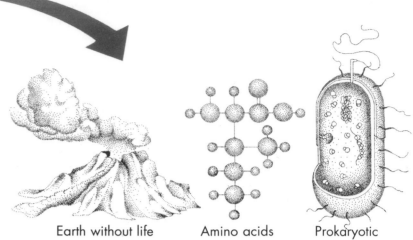

Earth without life   Amino acids   Prokaryotic cell

1

1. Imagine millions of volcanoes spewing out rivers of fiery rock and a surface pockmarked with craters that formed when meteorites struck. The atmosphere lacked oxygen, and there was no life at all. This was the Earth 4.6 billion years ago.
2., 3. Depending on the way they form, rocks are divided into three types—igneous, sedimentary, and metamorphic. Igneous rock forms as magma cools, and makes up the Earth's crust. In time igneous rock can be broken down by wind, water, glaciers, or plants, to form sediment, or small bits of rock and dust. Over thousands of years this sediment may be packed together, turning it into sedimentary rock. In time, with heat and pressure, sedimentary rock may be changed into metamorphic rock. From left to right, red granite (igneous rock) and serpentine.
4. A meteorite found in Mexico.

2

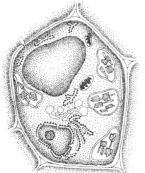
Plant cell

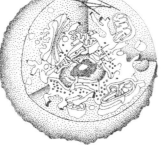
Animal cell

DNA

Species

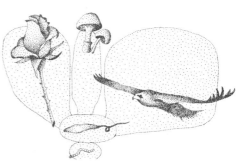
Five Kingdoms

3   4

THE BEGINNING OF LIFE

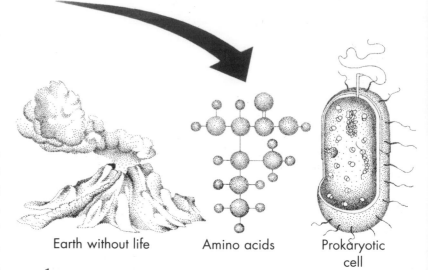

Earth without life Amino acids Prokaryotic cell

1

As the steaming Earth cooled, volcanoes continued to erupt, spitting out their gaseous mixture. The gases rose up and formed large clouds above the Earth. Away from the Earth's heat, the clouds began to cool. As the gases cooled, clouds of water vapor changed into liquid water, raining back onto the Earth's surface. Water began to pool on the crust, forming the first oceans. Water also pooled in smaller, low areas that had been formed by meteorites. Meteorites crashed into the Earth's surface, forming huge craters that were now filling with water.

The first forms of life may have appeared in the relatively shallow edges of the oceans, in lagoons, or in the smaller, separate pools of water. Here sunlight filtered through the water and supplied energy for chemical reactions. Many different chemicals were present in the water, and when energy was added, this "primordial soup" could have yielded amino acids. **Amino acids** are small chemical units that combine to form **proteins**, the main building blocks of living things. With a continuing supply of energy from the sun, proteins and other complex molecules could have come together to form the first simple living organisms—living things that could grow and reproduce.

1. Once the Earth began to cool, oceans began to cover large areas of the Earth's surface. Here chemicals triggered by lightning and solar energy began to react with each other, forming complex molecules. Some of these molecules were amino acids.
2. An amino acid molecule is made up of a long chain of carbon and nitrogen atoms linked together, as shown here.

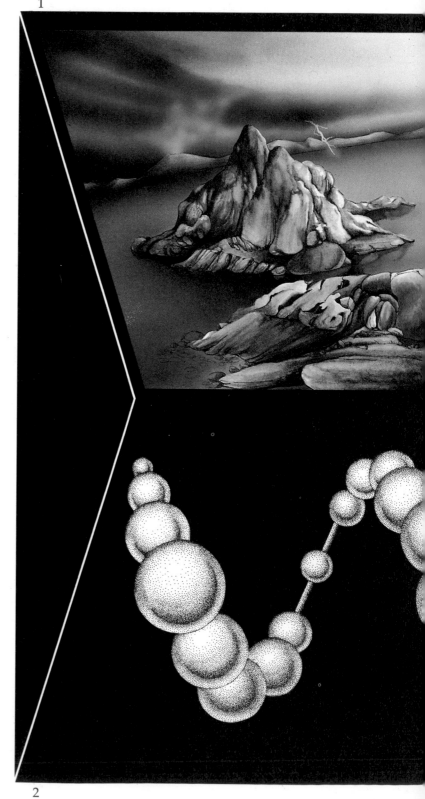

2

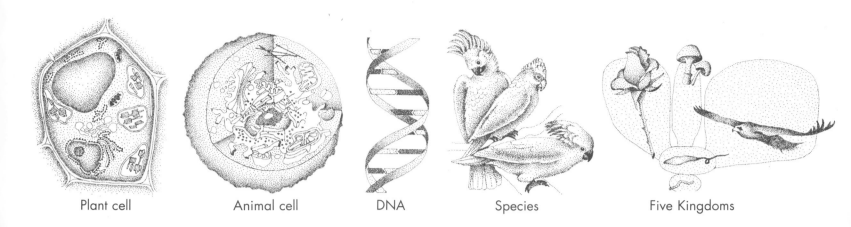

Plant cell   Animal cell   DNA   Species   Five Kingdoms

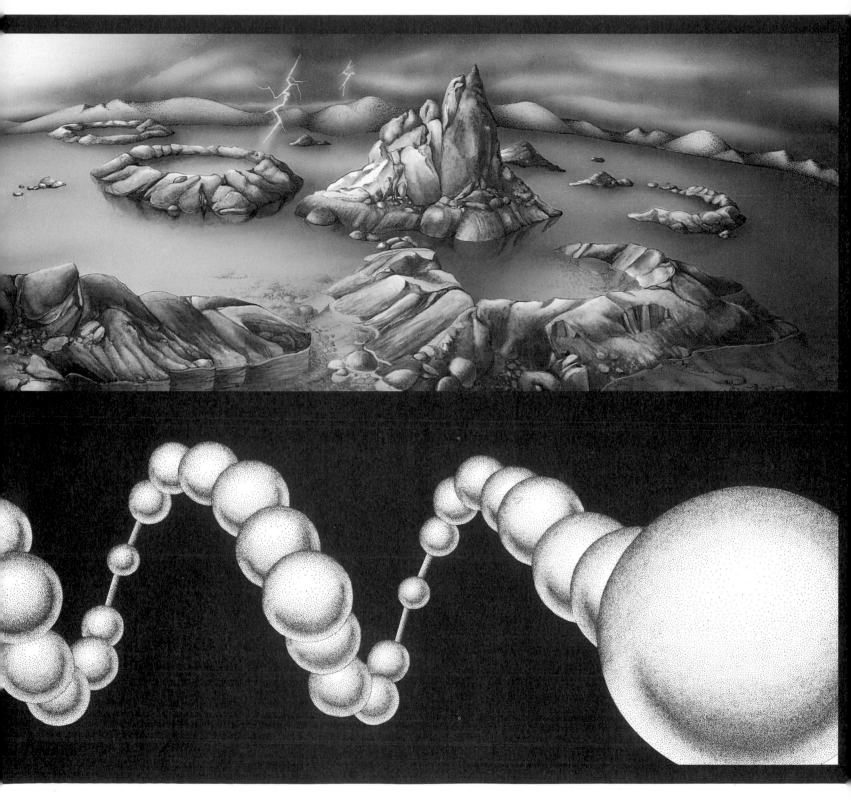

THE BEGINNING OF LIFE—OTHER IDEAS

Many scientists think that chemical reactions within a "primordial soup" led to the beginning of life. But this is only one hypothesis that explains the origin of life.

Another hypothesis suggests that life began not in a watery "primordial soup," but in a type of clay that formed the drier parts of the Earth's surface. The clay dust, found in rocks of the early Earth, contained many different molecules. These molecules reacted to form more complex molecules, including some that could develop into living things. Although this hypothesis is not widely accepted, some scientists believe it is the closest description of the origin of life.

A third hypothesis suggests that life began neither in pools of water nor on clay, and not even on Earth, but in outer space. Life may have started in large clouds of dust and gas floating between galaxies. Within the clouds, microorganisms—very small living organisms were formed. Comets could then carry these little organisms to Earth.

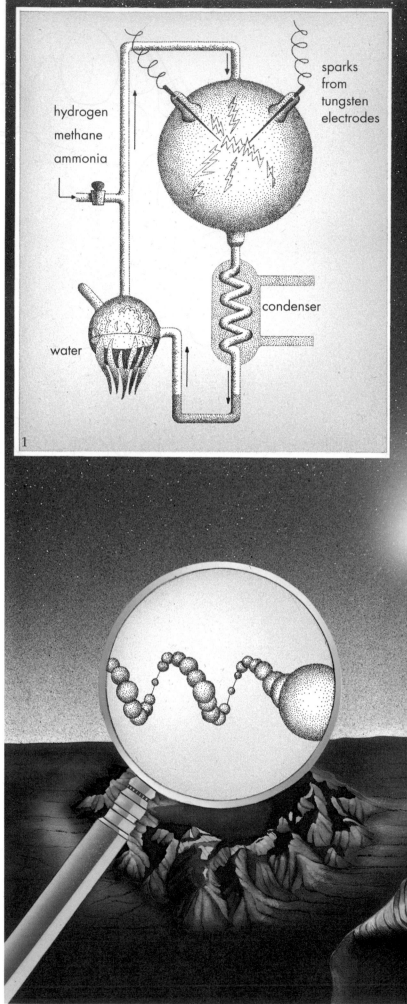

1. An American scientist, Stanley Miller, designed an experiment to prove that molecules of living organisms could be formed in a "primordial soup." In an experiment shown in the diagram above, Miller used water, hydrogen, methane, ammonia, and electric sparks to make amino acids and other complex carbohydrates.
2. The English astronomer Fred Hoyle suggested that life was brought to Earth by a comet that fell on the Earth's surface. Inside the nucleus of the comet, there may have been a watery environment that could protect these cells.
3. The French biologist, Antoine Danchin, suggested that life began not in a "primordial soup" but in rocks as organic molecules joined together.

THE FIRST CELLS

The first living things were very simple, single-celled organisms. These simplest of cells are all around us, floating in oceans and ponds, suspended in air, living in steaming sulfurous hot pools, even flourishing inside our own bodies. These simplest living things are **bacteria**.

Bacteria are simple and tiny, so small that they are invisible without a microscope. The simple, single cell of a bacteria, called a **prokaryotic cell**, is not organized like the cells of all other types of living things. Prokaryotic cells have few structures inside their cell membrane. Unlike other cells, prokaryotic cells do not have a **nucleus**. Instead, their DNA or other genetic material is attached to the cell membrane. The activities of the cell are directed by this DNA. The DNA or other genetic material carries instructions for the appearance and makeup of a living thing.

Traces of bacteria have been found in rocks that are 3.5 billion years old. These simple organisms are believed to be the ancestors of all other types of living things. From these simple cells, all other organisms evolved. One large group of bacteria, the blue-green bacteria, is believed to be the ancestor of all plants.

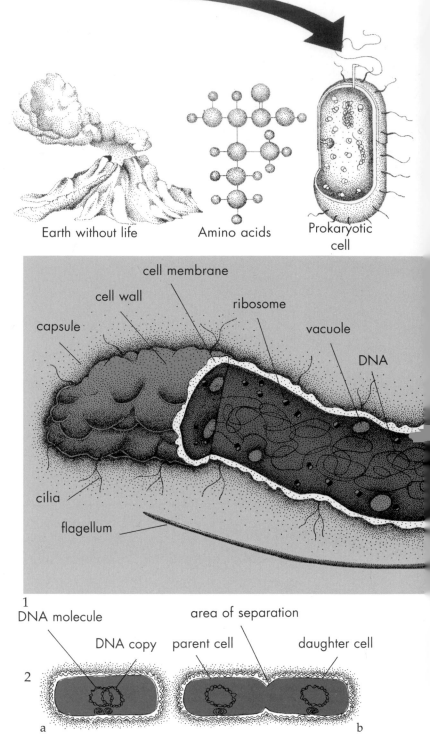

Earth without life   Amino acids   Prokaryotic cell

cell membrane
cell wall
ribosome
capsule
vacuole
DNA
cilia
flagellum

1
DNA molecule
DNA copy   parent cell   area of separation   daughter cell
2
a   b

1. Bacterial cells may be surrounded by several layers. The outermost layer is a capsule. Within the capsule, a cell wall surrounds the cell membrane, and the membrane surrounds the cytoplasm. A molecule of DNA (the genetic material), ribosomes, and vacuoles (fluid-filled sacs) are suspended within the cytoplasm. On the outer surface of the cell, cilia (small hairlike structures) wave back and forth. Long, whiplike structures called flagella, found in some bacteria, can move the cell through water.

2. When a bacteria cell reproduces, one cell splits to form two new cells. Before reproduction can occur, the DNA must replicate, or copy itself. Each new cell gets an identical copy of the DNA molecule.

3. These stromatolites from Shark Bay, Australia, are similar to those that lived billions of years ago. Stromatolites are thick mats formed of bacteria, blue-green bacteria, and sand. The mats build up as sand adheres to a sticky substance given off by the organisms. When the bacteria are covered by sand, they move up through the sand and again attract more sand; in this way they form new layers and large structures.

4. Blue-green bacteria differ in their appearance and structure from other bacteria. Only blue-green bacteria contain chlorophyll, the molecule that captures the sun's energy.
a. *Nitrobacter winogradskyi* **b.** *Desulfovibrio desulfuricans*
c. colony of *Streptomyces rimosus* **d.** *Micrococcus radiodurans*
e. *Rhodomicrobium vannielii* **f.** *Anabaena* is a blue-green bacteria. **g.** a spirochete.

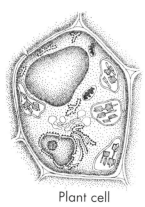

Plant cell

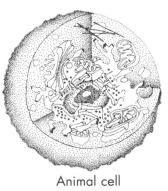

Animal cell

DNA

Species

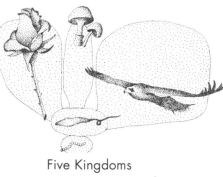

Five Kingdoms

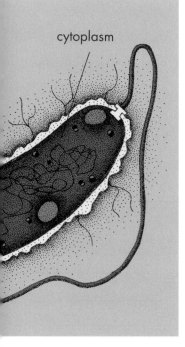

cytoplasm

3

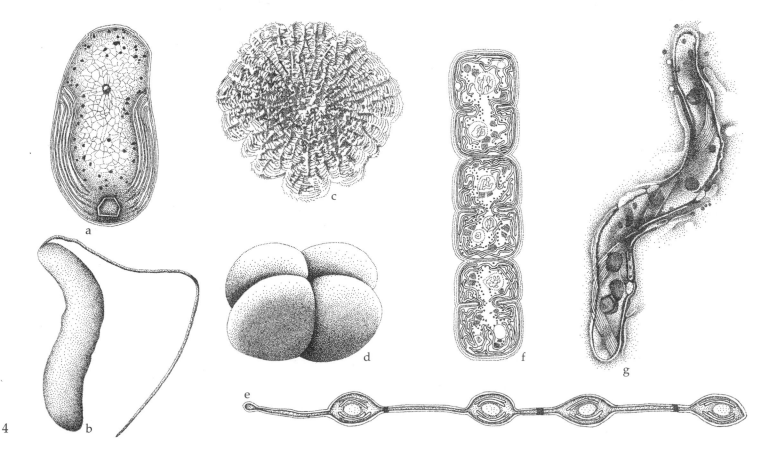

4

a

b

c

d

e

f

g

17

THE ORIGIN OF EUKARYOTIC CELLS

When you think of a living thing, you may think of a person, a rose bush, a mushroom, or even an amoeba. All of these organisms have one thing in common—they are made up of one or more eukaryotic cells. A **eukaryotic** cell has one main difference from the prokaryotic cell of the bacteria. As you saw, the DNA of a prokaryotic cell is attached to the cell membrane. In eukaryotic cells—whether an amoeba cell or a human cell—the DNA is enclosed within the nucleus.

Eukaryotic cells evolved from prokaryotic cells. Some prokaryotic cells that had lived on their own may have combined to form a larger new organism having a single, more complex cell. The former prokaryotic cells became the various **organelles**, structures of the cell of the new complex eukaryotic cell.

The evolution of eukaryotic cells was a momentous event, allowing a great diversity in future generations of organisms. It was followed by the evolution of multicellular organisms. The first organisms having many cells were colonies in which all cells were similar and had similar functions. In time, more complex organisms evolved in which cells specialized for different functions.

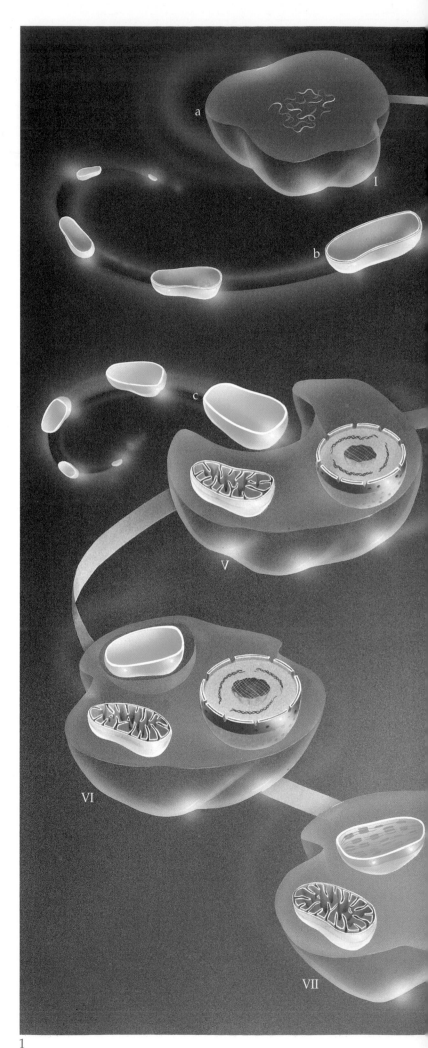

1. Eukaryotic cells are thought to have evolved from the union of prokaryotic cells. Steps I to III show different bacteria joining together. In Step IV, one bacteria cell transforms into a mitochondrion and the other into a nucleus. This cell, or something similar to it, eventually evolved into animal cells. In a separate evolution, this same type of cell was joined by a blue-green bacteria cell, which transformed into a chloroplast, shown in Steps V-VII. This type of eukaryotic cell evolved into plant cells.

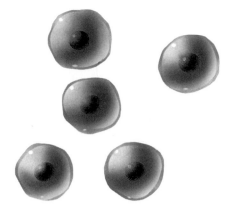

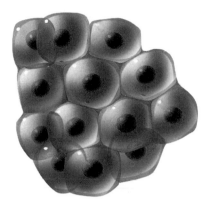

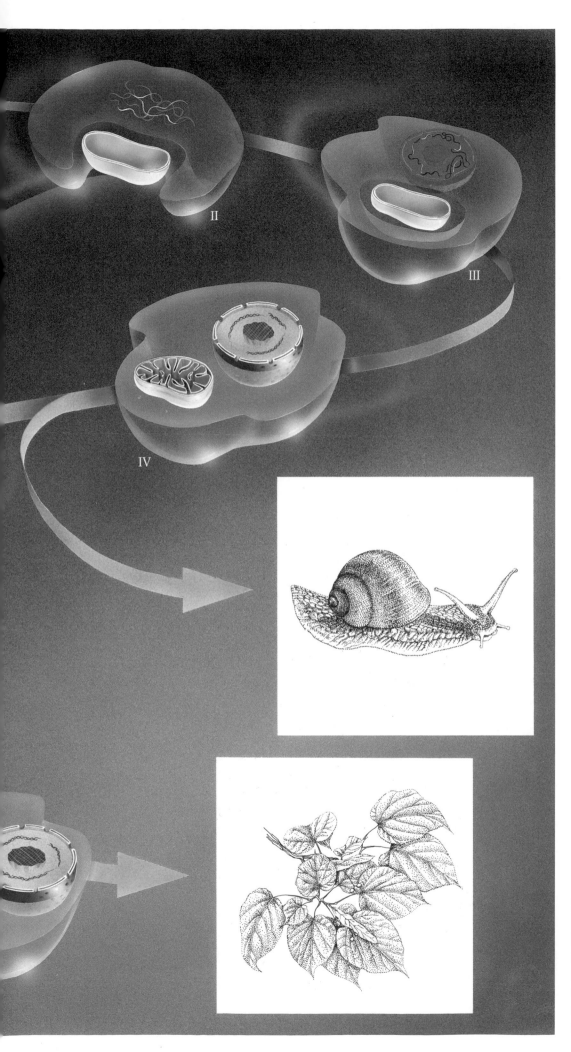

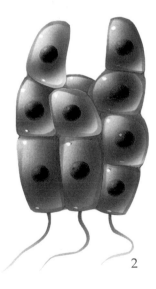

2. Eukaryotic cells joined together, forming colonies in which each cell had the same function. Later, cells specialized, with different cells having different functions. The specialized colony evolved into many-celled organisms, including plants, animals, and fungi.

PLANT CELLS

Photosynthetic algae are the oldest fossil evidence we have. These fossils date back to the Precambrian period, about 2.5 billion years ago. Plants developed on the Earth only in the Devonian period, about 395 million years ago.

Plants are important because they are producers. Unlike animals or fungi, they can make their own food. Plants make food by the process of photosynthesis. They capture light energy (from the sun) and transform it into chemical energy (in food), which is then available to other organisms. Photosynthesis is possible because plant cells contain the molecule **chlorophyll**.

When, photosynthesis began, more than 2 billion years ago, oxygen was released. Oxygen is a basic element in the atmosphere that makes animal life possible on Earth.

The first living things to contain chlorophyll and to make food were the blue-green bacteria. These simple cells had a profound impact on the Earth. The oxygen that they gave off as a waste product allowed animals and other types of organisms to thrive.

In time, some blue-green bacteria evolved into **chloroplasts**, the chlorophyll-containing structures found in cells of some types of protists and in plants. Although not all plant cells contain chloroplasts, they are one structure that shows the difference between plant cells and animal cells. Plant cells also have a cell wall. Cell walls surround the cell membrane and provide structure and support to plants, bacteria, and some other organisms. Plants also get structure from the large **vacuoles** that make up the largest part of many plant cells.

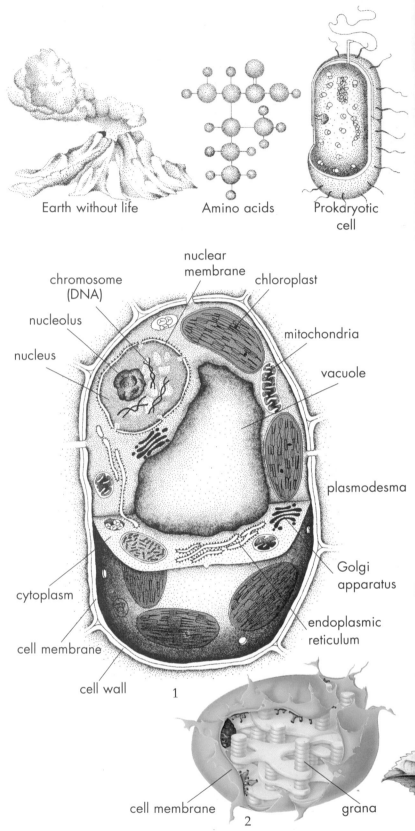

Earth without life   Amino acids   Prokaryotic cell

chromosome (DNA)
nucleolus
nucleus
nuclear membrane
chloroplast
mitochondria
vacuole
plasmodesma
Golgi apparatus
endoplasmic reticulum
cytoplasm
cell membrane
cell wall
1

cell membrane   grana
2

1. Plant cells have a cell wall that surrounds a cell membrane. Within the membrane many organelles are suspended within the cytoplasm.
2. Inside a chloroplast are structures that contain chlorophyll and that look like stacks of coins. Chlorophyll is a pigment, or colored matter, which absorbs energy from sunlight.

3., 4. Chloroplasts are found in cells that produce food. These cells are mainly found in the leaves but can also be located in other parts, such as in green stems. Cells containing chloroplasts are spread throughout the leaf of an apple tree. In the corn leaf, cells containing chloroplasts are clustered around the veins.

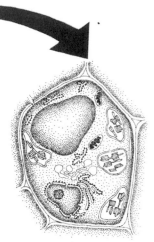
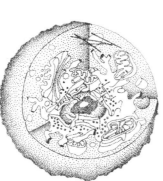
Plant cell

Animal cell

DNA

Species

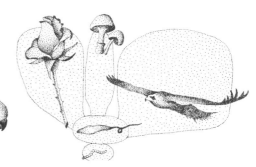
Five Kingdoms

stomate

epidermis

vein

chloroplast   photosynthetic cell

3

epidermis

stomate

vein

photosynthetic cell

chloroplast

4

ANIMAL CELLS

The oldest fossil remains that are said to be of animal organisms are the fauna of Edicara in Australia, which date back to about 640 million years ago.

All animals are consumers because animal cells do not have chloroplasts. Unlike plants that can produce their own food, animals must take in food. Animals also differ from plants and some other organisms in that animal cells do not have cell walls. In addition, vacuoles in animal cells are much smaller than in plant cells. Vacuoles in animal cells usually function to store material or to move wastes out of the cell.

Many of the other organelles are similar in animals and plants. A **cell membrane** envelops the cell and separates one cell from another. The cell membrane controls what moves into and out of cell. The cell membrane surrounds the **cytoplasm**, a watery substance in which the other organelles are suspended.

One organelle, the nucleus, directs activities of other parts of the cell. The nucleus is surrounded by its own membrane—the nuclear membrane. Inside the nucleus are **chromosomes** that contain DNA, the genetic material. As a cell divides to form two new cells, each one receives identical sets of chromosomes. Chromosomes and their DNA code for the production of all proteins.

1. An animal cell with organelles. (Not all of these organelles are found in every animal cell or at all times during the cell life cycle.) Starting at the outer surface of the cell is the cell membrane. Cell membranes are found in all animal cells. They surround the cytoplasm and separate one cell from the next. The nucleus, or control center of the cell, is divided into several parts. The nuclear membrane surrounds the nucleus and controls the flow of material into and out of the nucleus. The nucleolus makes and stores RNA, which is involved in making proteins. Chromosomes can be seen at certain times during the cell cycle. Mitochondria release energy from nutrients. Centrioles seem to play a part in the movement of chromosomes when the cell divides.
At the bottom of the cell you can see the endoplasmic reticulum. This is a folded membrane that extends through the whole cytoplasm and on which materials can travel through the cell. Endoplasmic reticulum can be covered with ribosomes, special structures on which proteins are made. The proteins may then be prepared for release from the cell by the Golgi apparatus. Lysosomes digest proteins and other material that may be harmful to the cell.

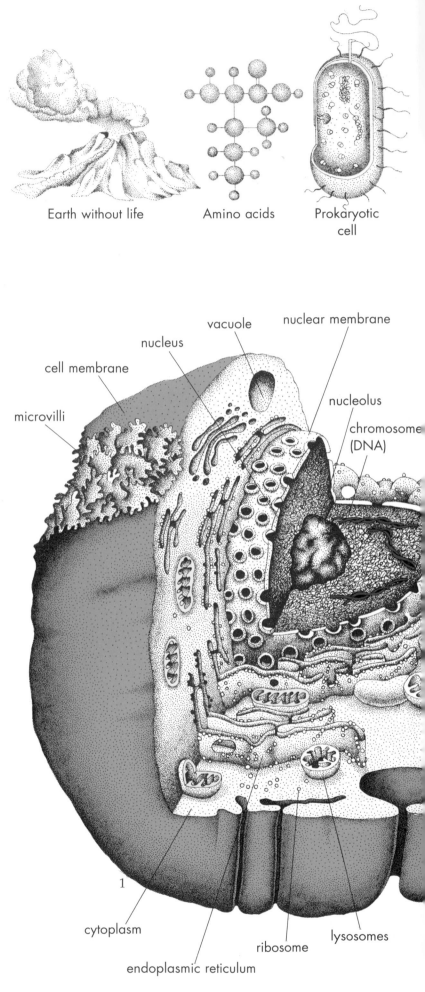

Earth without life

Amino acids

Prokaryotic cell

cell membrane

microvilli

nucleus

vacuole

nuclear membrane

nucleolus

chromosome (DNA)

cytoplasm

endoplasmic reticulum

ribosome

lysosomes

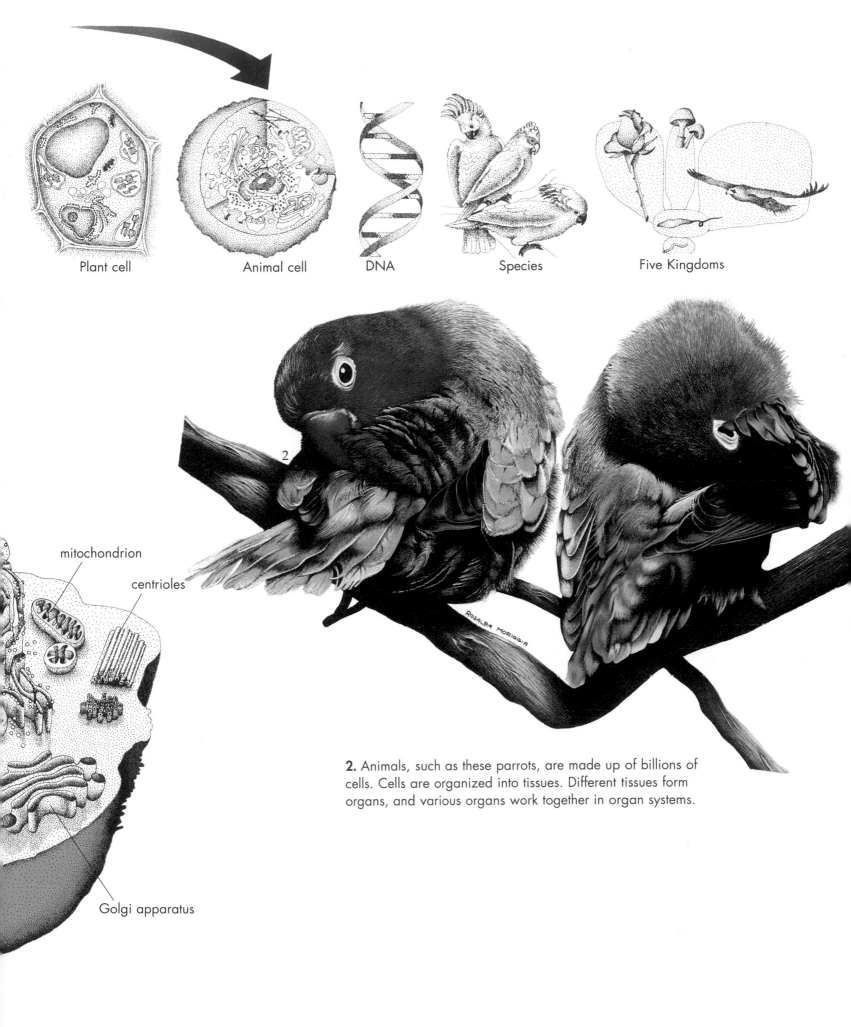

Plant cell

Animal cell

DNA

Species

Five Kingdoms

mitochondrion

centrioles

Golgi apparatus

2. Animals, such as these parrots, are made up of billions of cells. Cells are organized into tissues. Different tissues form organs, and various organs work together in organ systems.

DNA—THE CODE OF LIFE

How does a plant "know" how to bloom or drop its leaves? And what directs an animal to grow until it reaches a certain size? Living things are directed by a molecule that holds an incredibly detailed plan of life. This molecule is **DNA**.

DNA is a long, twisted molecule that is made up of thousands of small, simple molecules, called **nucleotides**. The nucleotides hook together like links in a chain. The order in which different nucleotides link up makes a code that directs the cell to make proteins. In this way DNA, the code of life, directs the activities of each cell in the body.

1. Inside the nucleus of the cell are many chromosomes. At a certain stage in the life of the cell, a chromosome looks like a fat letter *X*.
2. A chromosome is made up mainly of DNA, which can be tightly coiled and twisted together.
3. At a higher magnification, we would be able to see that DNA is actually two long chains that look like ladders twisting around each other in a spiral, or double helix. The two strands of this double helix are connected to each other by their nucleotides.
4. Each nucleotide molecule is made up of a sugar, a base, and a phosphate. Only certain bases will link to each other, as shown.
5. When a cell divides, each daughter cell (new cell) gets a full set of chromosomes. For this to happen, the DNA must replicate, or copy itself, before the cell divides. During replication, the hydrogen bonds holding the double helix are broken. Like a zipper, the two twisted chains of DNA pull apart from each other and serve as molds for a new strand. Two new double helixes will form, each having one strand of DNA from the original cell. The two new chromosomes will be identical.
6. DNA also serves as a set of directions for synthesizing, or making, proteins. The first step in protein synthesis is forming RNA. RNA moves out of the nucleus and into the ribosomes where proteins are synthesized. In a process similar to DNA replication, the DNA double helix separates and serves as a template for the RNA molecule called messenger RNA.

To produce protein, the molecule of DNA opens so that one of the two chains (a.) functions as a mold or model for the synthesis of one RNA molecule, ribonucleic acid. (b.) This RNA molecule will go from the nucleus to the cytoplasm where it will pass into the inside of the ribosomes. (c.) The bases of the RNA messenger will be read gradually by more RNA transfer molecules, (d.) each of which carries the amino acid (e.) corresponding to the bases that have been read.

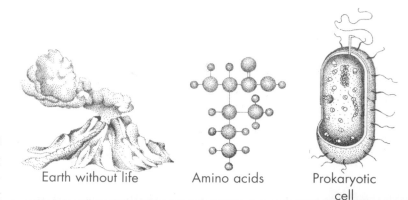

Earth without life   Amino acids   Prokaryotic cell

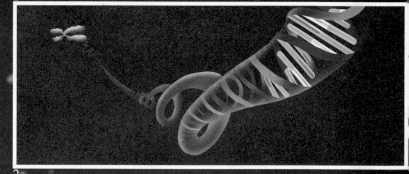

1

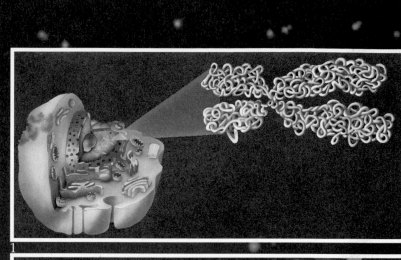

2

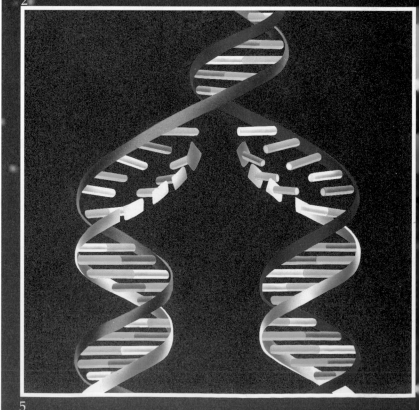

5

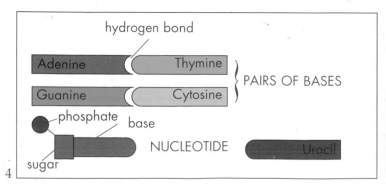

hydrogen bond

Adenine — Thymine
Guanine — Cytosine
} PAIRS OF BASES

phosphate   base
NUCLEOTIDE   Uracil
sugar

4

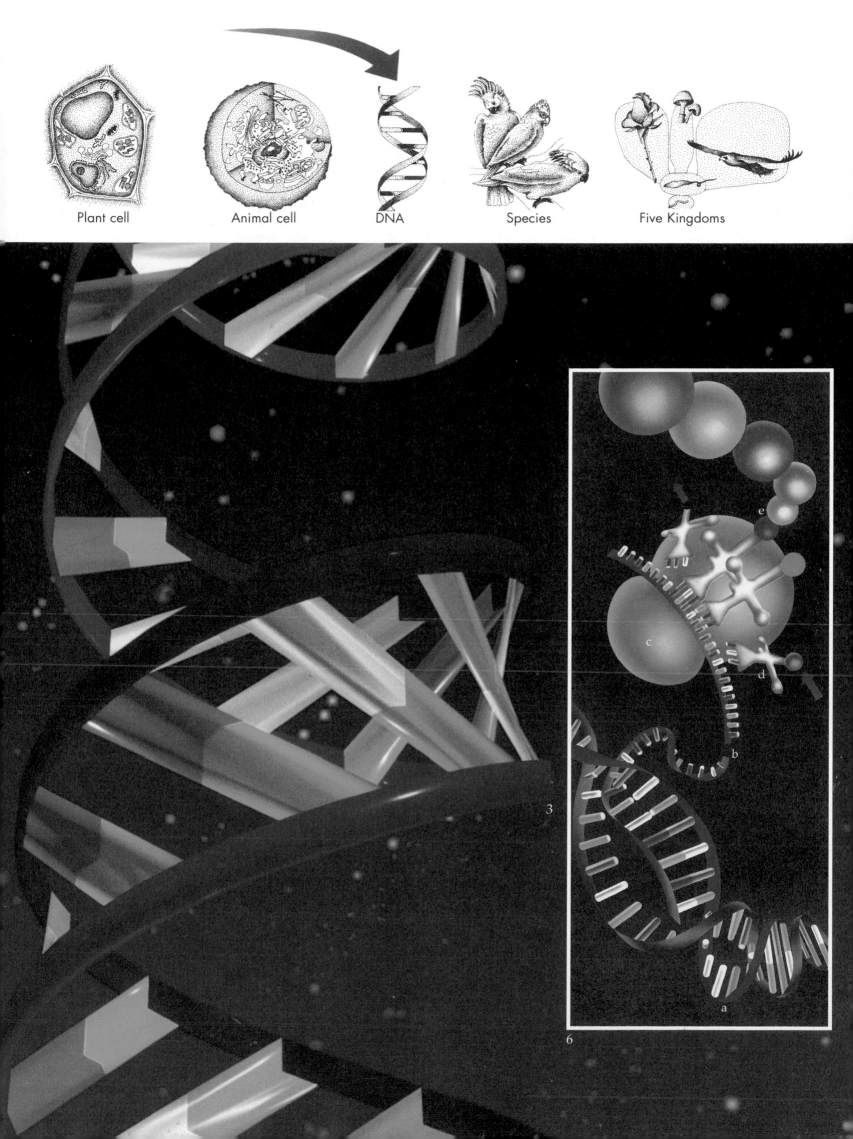

Plant cell

Animal cell

DNA

Species

Five Kingdoms

THE MECHANISM OF EVOLUTION

In the 1850s, an Austrian monk named Gregor Mendel studied the traits of pea plants. He made experiments using garden pea plants. Mendel chose pairs of traits or characteristics, such as height: short/tall; the surface of the seed: smooth/wrinkled; and flower color: red flowers/white flowers. In each experiment he crossed those plants that were different in only one of the pairs. They were alike in all other characteristics. From these experiments he discovered that one form of a trait is seen, and the contrasting form is hidden.

Scientists now understand the mechanism of traits being passed from one generation to the next. When a new individual is formed by sexual reproduction, it receives DNA from both of its parents. As you've learned, DNA directs cells of the body by coding for various proteins. Proteins in turn build the body, making it short or tall, blue-eyed or brown-eyed, potentially sick or well, and determining thousands of other traits.

When very simple organisms reproduce, one cell divides to form two new cells. This type of reproduction, involving only one parent, is called asexual reproduction. In this case the DNA copies itself and identical molecules of DNA go to each of the two new organisms. But what happens in sexual reproduction, which involves two parents? If the parents' DNA were simply copied and combined in the offspring, the offspring would have twice as much DNA as their parents. And the next generation would have twice as much again. This problem is avoided by a special type of division called **meiosis**, which precedes sexual reproduction. Meiosis results in the formation of special cells called gametes, which have half the usual amount of DNA or 23 chromosomes. Gametes—egg cells formed by the female and sperm formed by the male—then join together to form a new individual having the correct number of, or 46, chromosomes. In humans, gametes each have 23 chromosomes. When the gametes unite, they form the first cell of the new individual. This cell, and all other cells except gametes, will have 23 pairs, or a total of 46 chromosomes.

Gametes, or sex cells, are formed as a result of meiosis. In meiosis, a single cell divides to form four new cells. The drawing to the right shows stages of meiosis in a cell having only two pairs of chromosomes.
Steps of Meiosis: The chromosomes duplicate themselves (steps 1 through 5). Note that in meiosis, chromosomes cross over, forming new combinations (steps 2 and 3). A second division (steps 6 and 7) results in four new cells, each having half the usual number of chromosomes of the original cell.
Genetics and chromosomes determine many of the traits, such as hair and eye color, seen in these people.

mother   father

46
chromosomes
each

23   23   23   23

fertilization

7

THE THEORY OF EVOLUTION

Charles Darwin was a British naturalist who sailed around the world, studying plants and animals in distant lands. In five years of travel, he filled notebook after notebook with careful observations. Many of his important studies took place on the Galápagos Islands, off the coast of South America.

Darwin observed the slight differences among finches, a common bird in many parts of the world. Darwin noticed that the finches of the Galápagos Islands had various types of beaks. He also saw that the foods available on each island were different, and the beak of each type of bird was best-suited to the food that the bird ate. Based on these facts, Darwin suggested that the birds on each island had **adapted**, or changed over time, to suit their surroundings. He also suggested that, if this type of an adaptation resulted in a slight change, over a longer period of time there could be bigger changes. These bigger changes could result in a new **species**, a distinct group of living things that mate and have offspring.

Darwin theorized that a new species could **evolve**, or gradually change, from another species. But how could a group of living things change? How could a finch's beak change from one type to another? Darwin noticed that, although there were several main types of beaks, there were many smaller variations among the animals on each island. One beak might be slightly shorter, another might be slightly wider. Darwin suggested that this variety was the key. The variety might make one animal slightly better suited to its surroundings than the others. Those animals that were best-suited would be the healthiest. They would be the most likely to survive and to mate and produce offspring. This is referred to as natural selection and helps explain the theory of evolution.

1. An earlier scientist interested in the change in animals over time was Georges Cuvier. He studied the fossil remains of large animals, founding the science of paleontology. Cuvier asked why a certain type of animal might be found in one layer of rock and then disappear in the next layer. He suggested that a catastrophe, such as a meteorite (a), might totally kill off a population of animals. Later other animals might move into the area. Their remains would be found in higher layers of rock.

1

Catastrophe

a

Jean-Baptiste Lamarck

2

Charles Darwin

Evolution

parent

offspring

offspring

c

parent → parent

offspring

b

2. Another scientist studying fossils around the late 18th and early 19th centuries was Jean-Baptiste Lamarck. He studied fossils of small animals without backbones, such as mollusks. These fossils changed very gradually.

Lamarck's idea of how animals change over time was very different from Darwin's hypothesis. The most common example of Lamarck's theory is his explanation of how giraffes evolved long necks. We now know that this theory is incorrect and that acquired traits cannot be inherited.

3. In the illustration the theories of Lamarck and Darwin are compared, with the famous example of a giraffe. According to Lamarck, the giraffe's neck (b) grew long because of the effort the giraffe's ancestors made generation after generation to stretch their necks to reach for food on the highest leaves of trees. In every generation, thanks to the repeated stretching, their necks became a little longer, and this acquired feature became hereditary and was passed on to later generations.

According to Darwin's theory (c), in a population of giraffes where some have long necks and others short necks, natural selection, generation after generation, favored those with long necks because they were better able to get food. Those with short necks, which were unable to get food, died off until they finally became extinct. The sketch (c) summarizes Darwin's theory. A parent has children with different features: three with short necks and three with long necks. In later generations, we find one short-necked individual, two with medium-length necks, and three with long necks. As generations pass, only those individuals with long necks are chosen or selected while the others disappear.

FOSSILS—EVIDENCE OF EVOLUTION

How can we find out what really happened in the past—how we became what we are today? Darwin suggested answers based on his careful observations of animals around the world. Other scientists have looked at **fossils**, the traces or remains of once-living things. Animal fossils might be bones, shells, or even a trace of an animal, its footprint.

Fossils can form when an animal is trapped in something sticky and dies. For example, there are some places where tar forms and comes to the surface as large liquid pools. These look a little like a pool of water and attract many animals. Even large animals such as hairy mammoths can be trapped in the sticky tar. As they struggle to free themselves, they sink deeper and deeper, finally dying in the tar pit. Sometimes the bones of these large animals change little over time. These bones can be rebuilt into complete skeletons.

In other cases, animals may be trapped in sand pits. These animals also struggle and die. Then they may be covered by more sand. In time the sand may change to stone, and parts of the animal may also change to stone. Most often only the hard parts, such as shell, bones, or teeth, remain long enough to be preserved as stone. In other cases a softer part may decay while the stone forms, but an imprint may remain in the stone. Often this is the only type of plant fossil that can be found.

Sometimes very small animals, such as insects, are preserved in **amber**. Over long periods of time, amber can form from sap, the fluid that carries food material throughout a plant. Although most sap simply decays, a small fraction turns to amber and is valued as a gem. Amber that contains a fossil is rare and is highly valued.

1. Both plants and animals can be trapped in amber. Top row, from left to right on a diagonal: two leaves of a plant; a very rare amber containing a complete gecko (a type of lizard); leaves and petals of two different plants.
2. Second row, from left to right: Fossil shells of a type of cephalopod that lived millions of years ago and is now extinct. Cephalopods living today include the squid, octopus, and chambered nautilus. The fossils second and third from the right show crystals that formed.
3. Bottom two rows, from left to right on a diagonal: cross-sectional slices of fossilized trunks and stems.

Fossils trapped in amber
1

Fossil shells
2

Fossilized trunks
3

SPECIES

Much of what scientists know about the evolution of living things is based on the study of fossils. Many fossils reveal a sudden change in life forms during the Cambrian period. At this time, about 530 million years ago, huge numbers of different types of animals suddenly appeared in shallow ocean waters. In fact, there was such a sudden increase in numbers that this event is referred to as the "Cambrian explosion."

What caused the "Cambrian explosion?" One possible answer may be that conditions upon Earth became very favorable for life. Many different environments were available for the newly evolved multicellular organisms. These organisms were able to occupy the different environments. The result of adaptation to these environments was the evolution of many different species. These new species did not need to compete with others for either food or space.

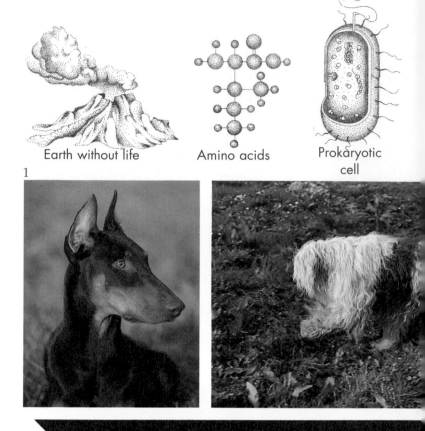

Earth without life   Amino acids   Prokaryotic cell

1

4

1. A species may be made up of living things—whether animals, plants, or fungi—that look very different from each other. For example, different breeds of dogs still belong to the same species. From left to right: Doberman pinscher, bobtail (sheepdog), bulldog, husky, blue Great Dane.

4. Donkey colt with its mother.
5. Horse colt with its mother.
6. Mule colt with its horse mother.

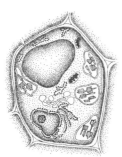
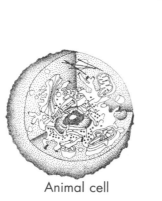

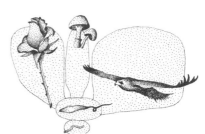

Plant cell   Animal cell   DNA   Species   Five Kingdoms

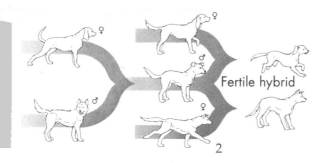

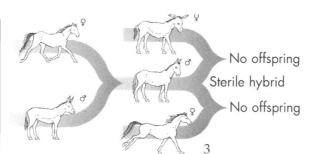

Fertile hybrid

2

No offspring

Sterile hybrid

No offspring

3

2. Although different dog breeds may look different, they still belong to the same species. Dogs from different breeds can mate and have offspring. These offspring can also mate and have offspring, too.

3. In contrast to animals from different breeds within the same species, horses and donkeys belong to different species. Although a horse and donkey can mate and produce mules, these mule offspring are completely sterile. Because mules cannot reproduce, donkeys and horses are defined as belonging to different species.

5   6

BIRTH AND DEATH OF SPECIES

Looking at the fossils of animals living millions of years ago, we see great numbers of species that no longer exist. These species are now **extinct**. What happened to them? What causes a species to become extinct or a new species to evolve? Often both extinction and evolution of species have the same cause—a change in the surroundings.

Sometimes a change in the environment is so great, that many species become extinct in one period of time. That may be over thousands of years. Such a great extinction is the well-known end to the dinosaurs 65 million years ago. There are many theories of the cause of this extinction. Some scientists have found evidence that an asteroid crashed on the surface of the Earth. Such a large strike could have sent tons of dust and ash into the air, blocking off sunlight for many months. Without sunlight, a large number of plants would have died. The animals that fed on the plants would have also died. But other scientists feel this mass extinction resulted from a more gradual change in the environment. Other evidence shows that climates were changing from warm and mild to less favorable or much colder conditions. Dinosaurs and other animals and plants which thrived in warmth, may have simply died off with the first frost and harsh winters.

As cold weather arrived at the end of the Cretaceous period 65 million years ago, animals that could control their body temperature were in a better position to survive.

3. *Thylacines*, an Australian mammal that became extinct in the 1960s.

4. The Whooping crane (*Grus americana*) is an endangered species. An endangered species is a species that has become rare and is in danger of becoming extinct. Often the danger is caused by humans changing a plant or animal's natural habitat.

1. New species can also evolve when animals are separated from their relatives. Common ancestors of both the zebra and giraffe may have been separated and isolated. As the animals adapted to their new and different environments, they could have evolved into new species. If none of the animals had been able to adapt to their new environment, the species would have died out and become extinct.

2. *Phacops rana*, a trilobite fossil found in Michigan. Trilobites are an extinct form of arthropod, or animal without a skeleton with a jointed body and limbs. They are one of the most common fossils of the Paleozoic era, evolving during the Cambrian period more than 600 million years ago and dying out in the great extinction at the end of the Permian period 225 million years later.

2

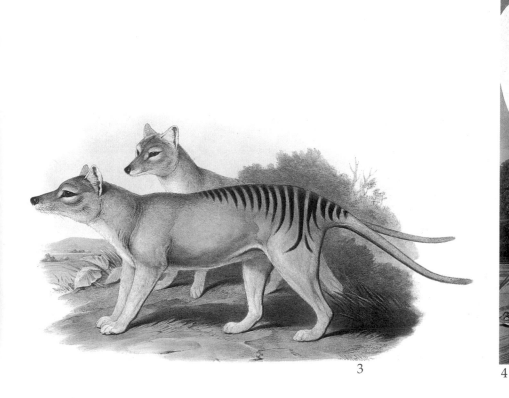

3

4

FIVE KINGDOMS

Earth without life   Amino acids

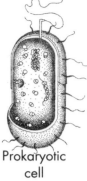

Prokaryotic cell

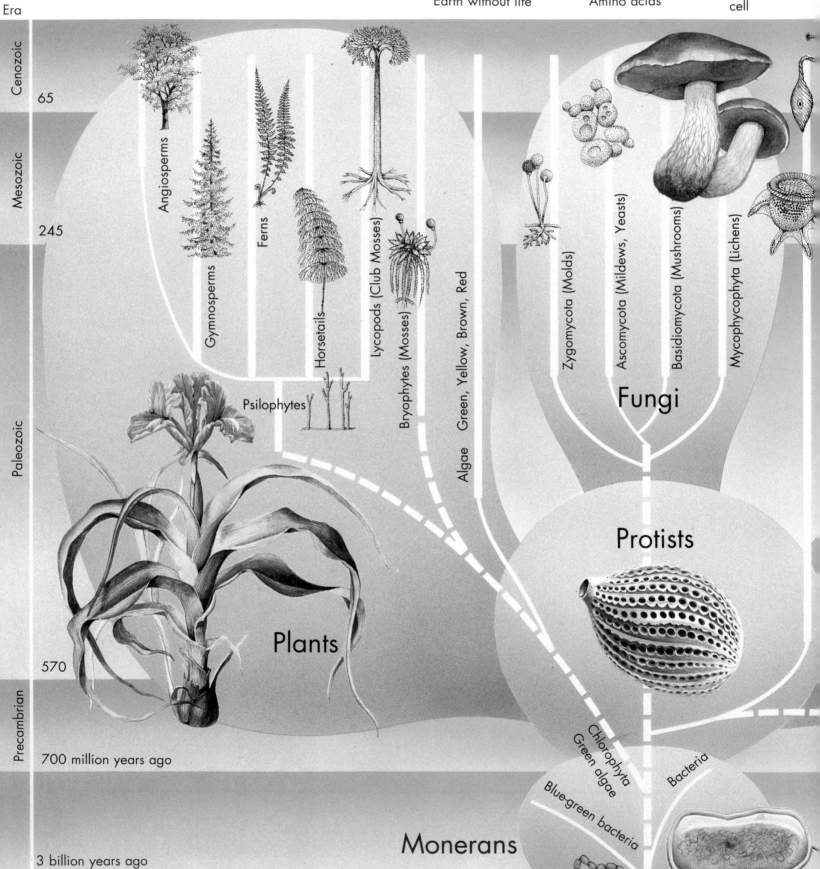

Era

Cenozoic

65

Mesozoic

245

Paleozoic

570

Precambrian

700 million years ago

3 billion years ago

36

Angiosperms

Gymnosperms

Ferns

Horsetails

Lycopods (Club Mosses)

Bryophytes (Mosses)

Psilophytes

Algae   Green, Yellow, Brown, Red

Zygomycota (Molds)

Ascomycota (Mildews, Yeasts)

Basidiomycota (Mushrooms)

Mycophycophyta (Lichens)

Fungi

Plants

Protists

Chlorophyta
Green algae

Bacteria

Blue-green bacteria

Monerans

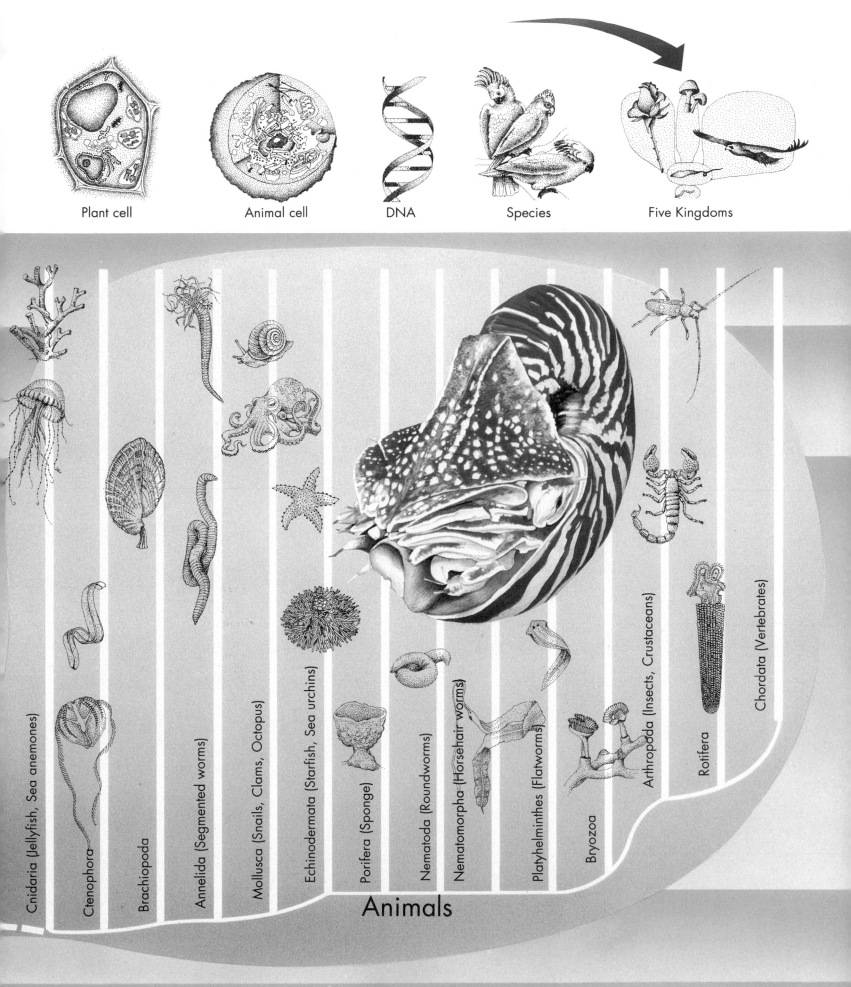

Plant cell   Animal cell   DNA   Species   Five Kingdoms

Cnidaria (Jellyfish, Sea anemones)

Ctenophora

Brachiopoda

Annelida (Segmented worms)

Mollusca (Snails, Clams, Octopus)

Echinodermata (Starfish, Sea urchins)

Porifera (Sponge)

Nematoda (Roundworms)

Nematomorpha (Horsehair worms)

Platyhelminthes (Flatworms)

Bryozoa

Arthropoda (Insects, Crustaceans)

Rotifera

Chordata (Vertebrates)

Animals

In general, simple living things evolved into more complex living organisms. Although scientists cannot find all the direct links in fossil studies, many links can be made by examining and comparing organisms. Scientists use many means, including looking at the form, comparing the anatomies, and using microscopes and biochemical studies. Organisms have been classified into five large kingdoms.

37

THE FIVE KINGDOMS TODAY

Animals

Monerans

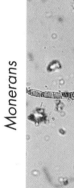

1

Protists

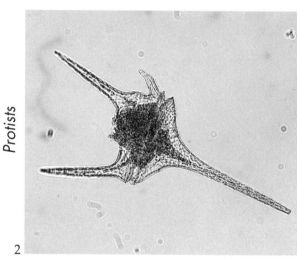

2

Fungi

3

Plants

4

For centuries scientists divided all living things into only two groups—plant and animal. But with the invention of the microscope, they found many differences within these groups. Now all living things are classified within five kingdoms. Here are examples of each of these kingdoms.

1. The long chain in the center is the blue-green bacteria *Oscillatoria rubescens*. The chain is made up of individual bacteria cells.

2. This tiny protist is *Ceratium hirundinella*. It is smaller than the period at the end of this sentence.

3. Certain types of fungi and algae can live together and benefit each other. This joint, living thing is called a lichen.

4. Seagulls are one of many examples from the animal kingdom.

5. Tropical plants, including banana and coconut palm trees, can be found in the Dominican Republic.

5

LIFE ON OTHER PLANETS

People have long wondered if life is found only on Earth. Could we find living things on another planet of the solar system?

Scientists know that all living things on Earth contain the element carbon. Carbon atoms are found in the basic building blocks of living things—proteins—and also in the master molecules of the cell—nucleic acids. Since carbon is plentiful in the universe, these same compounds that make up living things on Earth might be found on other planets.

Because Mars is in many ways similar to Earth, scientists have questioned whether life is possible on Mars. To answer this question, a spacecraft was sent to Mars. The *Viking I* showed that a very important compound—water—was lacking on Mars. And since all living things, as we know them, are made up in large part of water, there can be no life on Mars.

Scientists, however, are still open to the possibility that life in some form may exist in another part of our vast universe. However, since the distances are so great, it is most likely that if other living things do exist, we would never discover them.

1. The nine planets of the solar system drawn to scale. Mercury, at the top of the page, is the closest to the sun. Pluto, at the bottom of the page, is the farthest from the sun. Distances in the solar system are often measured in astronomical units. One astronomical unit is the average distance from the Earth to the sun. Because the sun is so large—its diameter is ten times as large as the diameter of Jupiter—only its edge is shown on the page.

2. The surface of Mars in sunlight. This photo was taken by *Viking I* when it came close to Mars' surface in 1976.

3. The Utopia plain of Mars, photographed by a *Viking I* probe. This probe explored the craters and canyons that could be seen before from a distance. Tests on samples of the Mars soil showed that the planet lacked any form of liquid water. Without water there can be no life as we know it.

1

Planet	Distance from sun (astronomical units)	Diameter	Maximum surface temperature	Most important atmospheric gases
Mercury	0.387	3015	430	?
Venus	0.723	7526	465	carbon dioxide nitrogen
Earth	1.000	7920	60	nitrogen oxygen water vapor
Mars	1.524	4216	20?	carbon dioxide nitrogen argon
Jupiter	5.203	88,700	-144	hydrogen helium
Saturn	9.539	75,000	-174	hydrogen helium
Uranus	19.18	29,000	-215	hydrogen helium
Neptune	30.06	28,900	-218	hydrogen helium
Pluto	39.44	≈1500	?	methane

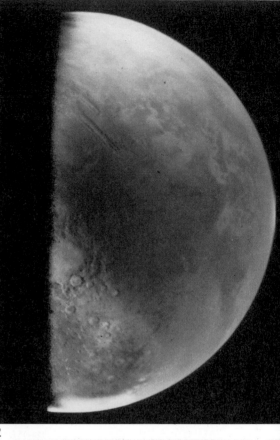

2

3

CONDITIONS NEEDED FOR LIFE

1. Surface temperature lower than the boiling point of water.
2. Presence of an atmosphere.
3. Presence of gravity strong enough to hold common gases, including carbon dioxide, water vapor, and oxygen.
4. Solar energy needed for photosynthesis.
5. Water in a liquid state.

GLOSSARY

Adapt: to change over time to better suit the surroundings.

Amber: fossilized sap, the fluid that carries material throughout a plant. Although most sap simply decays, a small fraction turns to amber and is valued as a gem.

Amino acids: small molecules that link together to form proteins.

Atmosphere: the gases that surround the Earth or other planets.

Bacteria: simple living things made up of a single prokaryotic cell.

Cell membrane: a structure that envelops the cell and separates one animal cell from another.

Chlorophyll: a molecule that absorbs sunlight, changing light energy to chemical energy, which supplies the energy needed for photosynthesis.

Chloroplasts: structures that contain chlorophyll. These are found in the cells of some protists and in plants.

Chromosomes: structures, sometimes visible in a cell, that contain DNA, the genetic material. As a cell divides to form two new cells, each one receives identical sets of chromosomes.

Cytoplasm: a watery substance in which other organelles of a cell are suspended.

DNA (Deoxyribonucleic Acid): a long, twisted molecule made up of many smaller molecules called nucleotides. DNA can be thought of as a code that directs the activities of a cell.

Endangered species: a species that has become rare and is in danger of becoming extinct. Often the danger is caused by humans changing a plant or animal's natural habitat.

Eukaryotic cell: a complex cell found in protists, plants, animals, or fungi; this cell has its genetic material enclosed within a nucleus.

Evolve: to change gradually. Over time living things can evolve.

Extinct: no longer living. Most species of organisms that lived in the past are now extinct.

Fossils: the traces or remains of once-living things. Animal fossils might be bones, shells, or even the trace of an animal, such as its footprint.

Gene: a part or segment of a chromosome. Genes determine the traits of an organism.

Hybrid: the offspring of the mating of two different species.

Igneous rock: rock that forms as magma cools, and probably makes up the Earth's crust.

Mammoth: extinct elephant.

Meiosis: a special type of division that precedes sexual reproduction. Meiosis results in the formation of special cells called gametes, which have half the usual amount of DNA.

Metamorphic rock: rock that forms over time from sedimentary rock, with heat and pressure.

Nucleotide: a molecule made up of a sugar, base, and a phosphate group. RNA and DNA are chains of nucleotides.

Nucleus: the structure that directs the activities of the cell and that contains the DNA or other genetic material.

Organelles: structures of a cell.

Prokaryotic cell: a simple cell that has structures and that does not have a nucleus, the structure that directs the activities of the cell.

Protein: building block of the cell. Proteins are made up of amino acids.

RNA (Ribonucleic Acid): a large molecule similar to DNA. RNA is involved in the production of proteins within the cell.

Sedimentary rock: rock made up of sediment, or small bits of rock and dust, that has packed together and hardened into rock over time.

Species: a distinct group of living things that mate and have fertile offspring. Animals from two different species cannot produce fertile offspring.

Vacuoles: fluid-filled sacs found in plant and animal cells.

FURTHER READING

Bailey, Marilyn. *Evolution: Opposing Viewpoints.* Greenhaven, 1990

Balkwill, Fran. *DNA is Here to Stay.* Carolrhoda, 1993

Byczynski, Lynn. *Genetics: Nature's Blueprints.* Lucent, 1991

Edelson, Edward. *Genetics and Heredity.* Chelsea, 1991

Gamlin, Linda. *Evolution.* Dorling Kindersley, 1993

Hooper, Tony. *Genetics.* Raintree Steck-Vaughn, 1993

Stephenson, Robert and Browne, Roger. *Exploring Variety of Life.* Raintree Steck-Vaughn, 1992

INDEX

EVOLUTION OF THE MONERAN, PROTIST, PLANT, AND FUNGI KINGDOMS

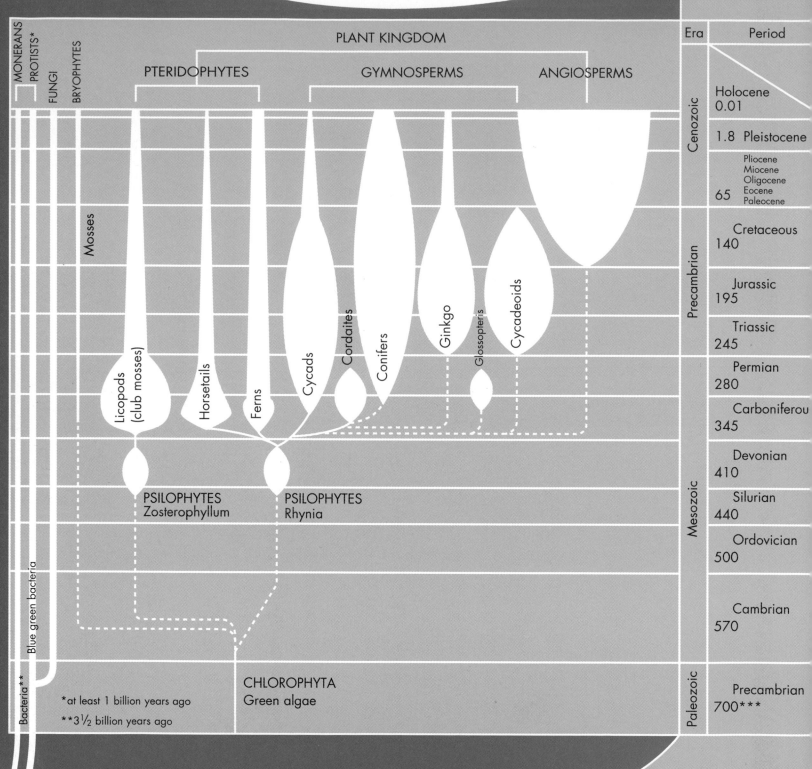

MONERANS

PROTISTS*

FUNGI

BRYOPHYTES

PLANT KINGDOM

PTERIDOPHYTES

GYMNOSPERMS

ANGIOSPERMS

Mosses

Licopods (club mosses)

Horsetails

Ferns

Cycads

Cordaites

Conifers

Ginkgo

Glossopteris

Cycadeoids

PSILOPHYTES
Zosterophyllum

PSILOPHYTES
Rhynia

Blue green bacteria

Bacteria**

CHLOROPHYTA
Green algae

*at least 1 billion years ago

**3 1/2 billion years ago

Era	Period	
Cenozoic	Holocene	0.01
	Pleistocene	1.8
	Pliocene Miocene Oligocene Eocene Paleocene	65
Precambrian	Cretaceous	140
	Jurassic	195
	Triassic	245
	Permian	280
	Carboniferou	345
Mesozoic	Devonian	410
	Silurian	440
	Ordovician	500
	Cambrian	570
Paleozoic	Precambrian	700***

EVOLUTION OF THE PROTIST AND ANIMAL KINGDOMS

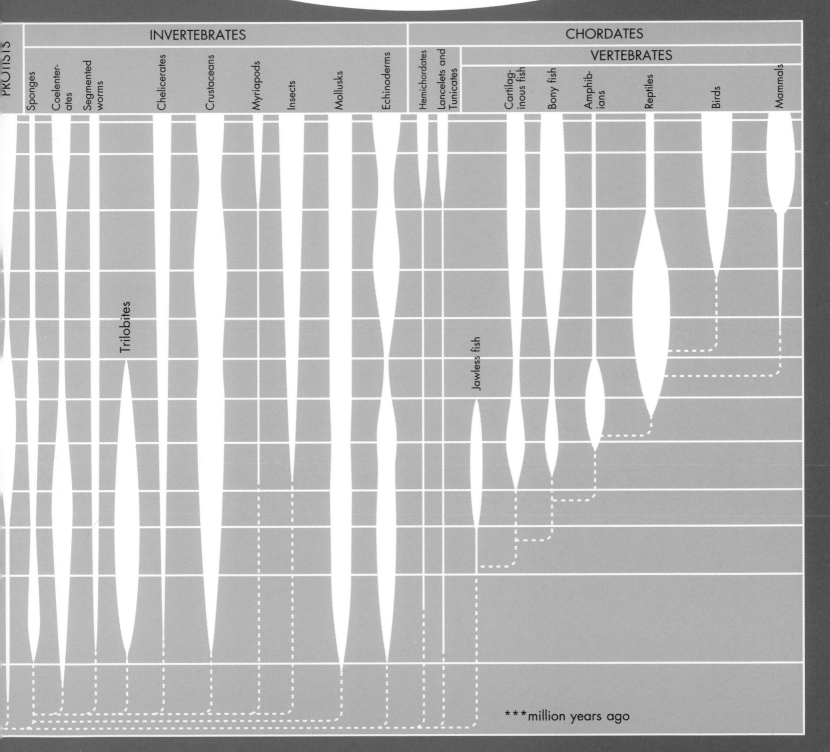

PROTISTS

INVERTEBRATES

CHORDATES

VERTEBRATES

Sponges
Coelenterates
Segmented worms
Chelicerates
Crustaceans
Myriapods
Insects
Mollusks
Echinoderms
Hemichordates
Lancelets and Tunicates
Cartilaginous fish
Bony fish
Amphibians
Reptiles
Birds
Mammals

Trilobites

Jawless fish

***million years ago